WEATHER
AND SEASONS

By Jillian Powell

New York

Published in 2015 by The Rosen Publishing Group, Inc.
29 East 21st Street, New York, NY 10010

Series editor: Amy Stephenson
Series designer: Jeni Child
Crafts: Rita Storey
Craft photography: Tudor Photography
Picture researcher: Diana Morris

Picture credits:
AlaskaStock/Alamy: 20t. Guido Amrein Switzerland
Shutterstock: 26-27bg, 31t. Andia/Photoshot: 24tr. Galyana
Andrusko/Shutterstock: 14-15 bg. Blueskystudio/Shutterstock:
6-7bg. Ronald Caswell/Shutterstock: 22-23 bg. Clover
Photoshot: 16tr Creative Travel Projects/Shutterstock: 1.
Digoarpi Shutterstock: 4bl. Ehp73/istockphoto: 18t. Lane
V Erikson/Shutterstock: 4br. J P Forte/istockphoto: 11t
David R Frazier/Alamy: 11b. Robert Harding PL/Alamy: 15t.
Irink/Shutterstock: 16tl. Joruba/Dreamstime: 23b. Joyfull
Shutterstock: 16c. KarimKamon/Shutterstock: 32b. Katrina 1/
front cover tr. Kemeo/Shutterstock: 8cl. Alan Kiehr Alamy: 27t.
Lucyna Koch/istockphoto: 20b. nicky-m/istockphoto: 16tc.
Mallivan/istockphoto: 15b. Andrew Mayovskyy/Shutterstock:
7b. Aliaksander Mazurkevich/Dreamstime: 8cr Vasiliy
Merkushev/Shutterstock: 14b. Mikkolem/Dreamstime:5t Dan
Mirica/Shutterstock: 16bl. Olga Mittsova/Shutterstock:18-19bg.
Zoltan Mucsi Shutterstock: front cover c. Marvin Nauman/
UPPA/Photoshot: 26b. Nadav Neuhaus/WpN/Photoshot: 18b.
Alexandra Nika/Shutterstock: 23t. Noppharat/Shutterstock: 10c.
Paul Orr/Shutterstock: 10-11 bg. Bill Perry/ Shutterstock: 12t.
photographerlondon/Dreamstime: 19t. Radoiu/Dreamstime:
30 Redeyed/Dreamstime: 22b Michael Schmeling/Dreamstime:
7t. Mark Sisson/FLPA: 8r. Solarseven/Shutterstock: 27b. Stanny/
Shutterstock: 16cr. Stockelements/Shutterstock: 12b. Swa182/
Shutterstock: 28t thehague/istockphoto: 5c. Tinors/istockphoto:
22t. Lily Trott/Shutterstock: 8l. Nickolay Vinokurov/Shutterstock:
24cl. wikipedia: 6b.

Library of Congress Cataloging-in-Publication Data

Powell, Jillian, author.
 Projects with weather and seasons / by Jillian Powell.
    pages cm. — (Make and learn)
 Includes index.
 ISBN 978-1-4777-7181-5 (library binding) —
 ISBN 978-1-4777-7182-2 (pbk.) —
 ISBN 978-1-4777-7183-9 (6-pack)
 1. Handicraft—Juvenile literature. 2. Weather—Miscellanea—
Juvenile literature. 3. Seasons—Miscellanea—Juvenile
literature. I. Title.
 QC981.3.P69 2015
 745.59—dc23
                        2014014573

Manufactured in the United States of America

CPSIA Compliance Information: Batch #WS14PK9: For
Further Information contact Rosen Publishing, New York, New York at
1-800-237-9932

CONTENTS

Some of the projects in this book require scissors, paint, glue, baby oil, a glue gun and a pin. We would recommend that children are supervised by a responsible adult when using these things.

WHAT CAUSES WEATHER?

We experience weather all of the time, but what makes it change from day to day?

The weather is always changing

Weather is caused by changes in the state of the Earth's **atmosphere**. This is the layer of gases that surrounds the Earth and makes up the air we breathe. These changes mean the weather can be hot, cold, wet, dry, windy or calm. Many other things help make weather, such as the air temperature, the speed of the wind and its direction and whether there is bright sunshine or a cloudy sky.

Weather vanes point in the direction the wind is blowing. This French vane is pointing west. (*Ouest* is the French word for west.)

Cold and wet weather can produce snowstorms or blizzards.

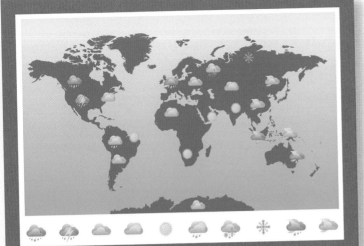

Symbols on this weather map tell us what the weather is like in different places around the world.

Weather maps

Weather **forecasters** use maps of a country or a place to tell us what the weather will be like there. They use symbols to show where it will be sunny or cloudy and where it might rain or snow. They can also show us information such as temperature, wind speed and direction and how the weather might change.

When areas of warm and cold air meet, they form warm or cold weather **fronts**. Warm air is lighter than cool air because it is less **dense**. When warm air rises, cool air will take its place below. This movement of warm and cold air creates changes in the weather.

Weather and us

Weather can affect lots of things, such as the clothes we wear and the outdoor activities or sports we do. It is important for farmers as they need the right amount of sun and rain for their crops to grow and produce a good harvest. The weather can also affect travel. Cars, buses, trains, ships and planes can be affected by bad weather, such as strong winds, fog, snow or heavy rain that causes flooding.

People enjoying the sunshine and hot weather on a beach.

Quick *FACTS*

• The weather is caused by changes in the Earth's atmosphere.
• It is always changing.
• It affects us and the things around us.

WEATHER AND SEASONS

The tilt of the Earth's axis as it travels around the Sun gives us our seasons.

All change

Just as the weather can change each day, it also changes with the seasons. The Earth takes one year to **orbit** the Sun. The Earth's **axis** is tilted at an angle so when one half (or **hemisphere**) of Earth is pointing towards the Sun, the other half is pointing away. The hemisphere that is pointing towards the Sun is in summer, the other hemisphere is in winter. The Earth also spins on its axis, which creates day and night. It takes 24 hours to complete each spin.

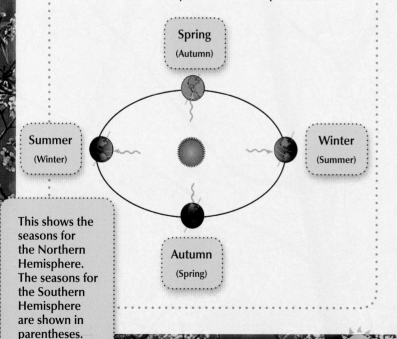

Spring
(Autumn)

Summer
(Winter)

Winter
(Summer)

Autumn
(Spring)

This shows the seasons for the Northern Hemisphere. The seasons for the Southern Hemisphere are shown in parentheses.

The seasons

In **tropical** regions, between the **equator** and the Tropic of Cancer or the Tropic of Capricorn, it stays warm all year. There are only two seasons, a wet and a dry season. In **temperate** regions, which lie between the tropics and the **polar circles**, there are four seasons. As Earth orbits the Sun, the hemisphere in summer gradually begins to tilt away from the Sun and its season changes from summer into autumn. As the other hemisphere begins to tilt towards the Sun, its season also changes, from winter into spring.

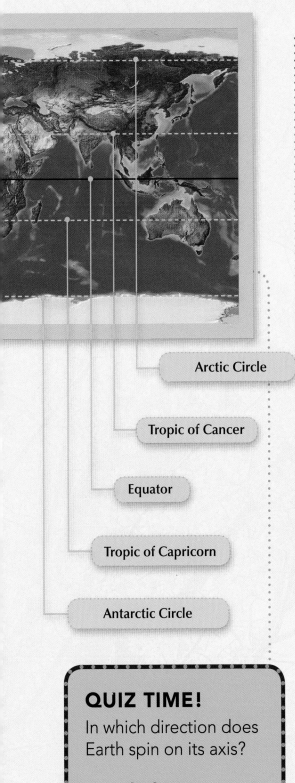

Arctic Circle

Tropic of Cancer

Equator

Tropic of Capricorn

Antarctic Circle

QUIZ TIME!

In which direction does Earth spin on its axis?

a. clockwise
b. counterclockwise
c. both

Answer on page 32.

The four seasons

In spring, the Sun begins to climb higher in the sky and it is daylight for longer. There is more sunshine and the air gets warmer. Summer is the warmest season because the Sun is at its highest in the sky. Summer has the most daylight hours, with long evenings.

In autumn, daylight gets shorter and the Sun begins to get lower in the sky. Less daylight means less Sun, so the air begins to get cooler. Cooler temperatures and damp air can make it misty or foggy in the mornings and evenings. As winter arrives, the Sun is at its lowest in the sky. There are fewer daylight hours, so the ground has less time to warm up. The temperature drops so it feels cold.

The Sun is much lower in the sky in the winter. Less daylight means it is colder.

? How do the seasons affect animals and plants?
Turn the page to find out.

Spring to summer

As the seasons change they affect living things around us. In spring, with more hours of daylight and warmer temperatures, trees and plants begin to grow. Buds open into flowers that bees and other insects will **pollinate**. Spring is also the time when many baby animals are born. Some birds and animals **migrate** with the seasons. Swifts and swallows fly from Africa to Europe for the summer, to find food and to breed.

Autumn leaves

In autumn, trees and plants begin to prepare for winter. **Evergreen** trees stay green all year but the leaves on **deciduous** trees and plants change color. The trees stop sending water to their leaves so the leaves begin to dry out and lose their green color. They turn red or yellow and then fall off the tree.

Lambs are usually born in the spring.

Baby swallows in their nest in the summertime.

Leaves turn red and yellow in the autumn.

A dormouse hibernating in a nest in the winter.

Winter hibernation

In winter, icy and snowy weather can make it hard for animals to find food and stay warm. Some animals hibernate, which means they find a warm and dry place and go into a deep sleep. They won't wake up again until the spring.

QUIZ TIME!

The colors found in natural things, such as leaves, are called:

    a. **pigtails**
    b. **pigments**
    c. **pigsties**

Answer on page 32.

Make This

Autumn leaves come in lots of beautiful colors. Make a seasonal wreath from fallen leaves to go on a door, or for an autumn display.

You could make a wreath for every season. What kinds of things could you find to put on a winter, a spring or a summer wreath?

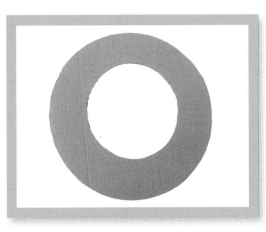

1 Carefully cut out a large ring from cardboard, or cut the centre out of a paper plate.

2 Glue on lots of autumn leaves. Keep overlapping them until the whole ring is covered.

3 Glue on acorns, berries and pine cones. Let dry.

4 Loop a piece of ribbon through the wreath. Hang it up.

SUNSHINE AND TEMPERATURE

The Sun warms the temperature of the air.

The Sun's energy

Every living thing on Earth needs the Sun's warmth and energy. The Sun is very hot – its surface is about 9,930 degrees Fahrenheit (5,500°C). The huge distance that sunlight has to travel through space to reach Earth and the Earth's atmosphere help to protect us from this fierce heat. The heat from the Sun warms up everything, including the air around us.

The Sun's energy warms up the Earth's land, water and air.

! WARNING: Never look directly at the Sun. It is so bright it can damage your eyes.

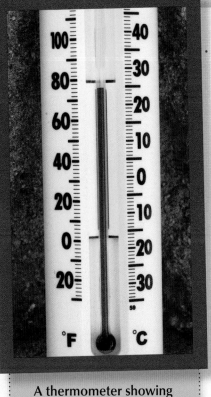

A thermometer showing that it is a warm day. The temperature is 76°F (26°C).

Measuring temperatures

Weather map symbols show the Sun with a number. This is the temperature in degrees Fahrenheit (°F) measured on a **thermometer**. When the air temperature rises, the liquid in a thermometer **expands** and moves up the scale. When it cools down again, the liquid **contracts** and moves back down the scale. When the temperature rises to 86°F (30°C), it feels hot. At around 59°F (15°C), it feels mild, and at 41°F (5°C) it is cold. If the temperature falls to 32°F (0°C), it is freezing.

Daily temperatures

The season and the position of the Sun in the sky both affect how warm the weather feels. As the Sun rises in the sky it begins to warm up the ground. Heat from the ground rises, which also helps to warm up the air temperature. The air is warmest in the early afternoon, when the Sun is high in the sky. At night, when there is no sunlight, it feels colder. The coldest time is usually just before sunrise.

Quick *FACTS*

• The air temperature changes with the seasons and the time of day.
• We often measure temperature in degrees Fahrenheit (°F).

? What else do you think affects the air temperature? Turn the page to find out.

Mountains, valleys and deserts

The air temperature is cooler in high places. On mountains, it drops by around 10°F (6.5°C) for every 3,200 feet (1,000 m) you climb. The air here feels cooler because it is often windy in high places. The air higher up is also thinner than air lower down and cannot hold the heat that rises from the ground. The hottest places on Earth are some **deserts** and low-lying dry valleys, such as Death Valley in California, where the temperature

Death Valley, in California, USA, is one of the lowest and hottest places on Earth.

can reach over 134°F (57°C). The coldest place on Earth is in Antarctica, which is also the world's biggest desert. Temperatures here stay below freezing all year round and can fall to around -128°F (-89°C).

A hot and sunny day in Central Park, in New York City.

Towns and cities

In towns and cities, the air temperature is usually warmer than in the country. This is because buildings store heat from the Sun during the day. As the air cools at night, the buildings release the stored heat into the air, raising the temperature.

Cool shade

Clouds, trees, buildings and sun umbrellas can all block out the Sun and give shade. Even on a hot day it feels cooler in the shade, because we are not feeling the heat from the Sun's rays directly upon us.

TRY THIS
Take a thermometer out on a sunny day and try taking readings in the sunshine and in the shade at different times of day. Make a bar graph to record your readings at set times.

Make This

The Sun's rays are blocked and reflected by this suncatcher. Notice what happens when you put it in bright sunlight and in a breezy spot.

You could experiment with different colors. Which colors produce the best effects?

1 Ask an adult to cut off the top section of a large plastic drink bottle. Paste torn pieces of tissue paper all over it with glue. Let dry.

2 Tape a piece of cling wrap to a table. Paste 3 or 4 layers of torn tissue paper all over it using watered-down white glue. Let dry.

3 Peel the tissue paper layer off the cling wrap. Using a jar lid to draw around, cut out lots of circles from the tissue paper layer.

4 Cut four lengths of string. Tape circles along each string. Tape the strings to the bottle top. Hang up your suncatcher near a window using more string.

RAINY WEATHER

Rain is part of the Earth's water cycle, and all living things need water.

All plants, animals and people, need water to live. The water cycle is the way the Earth's water is constantly recycled. As the Sun heats the water in rivers, lakes and oceans, water droplets **evaporate** and turn into **water vapor**. This vapor rises into the air and cools. As it cools, the water vapor **condenses**, turning back into tiny water droplets. The water droplets gather together to form clouds and as the droplets are blown around and bump into each other they get bigger. The clouds get bigger as the drops get larger and heavier, until the clouds can't hold any more and release them as rain.

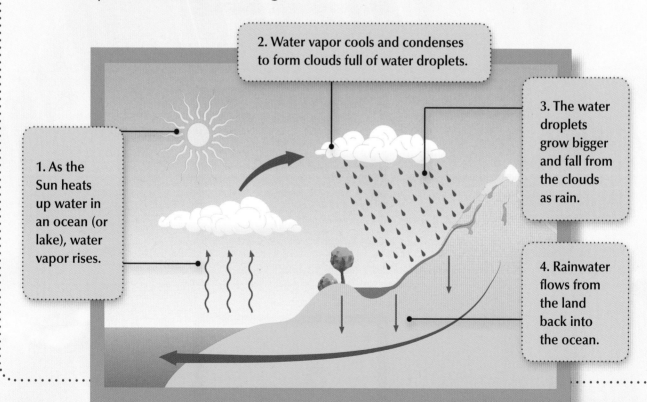

2. Water vapor cools and condenses to form clouds full of water droplets.

3. The water droplets grow bigger and fall from the clouds as rain.

1. As the Sun heats up water in an ocean (or lake), water vapor rises.

4. Rainwater flows from the land back into the ocean.

Quick FACTS
• All living things need water. • The Earth has only so much water, which it constantly recycles through the water cycle.

Rainfall

Rain that falls onto the land forms puddles. Some rain soaks into the ground and is taken up by the roots of plants. Some goes even deeper into rocks in the ground. Water that falls into rivers and streams flows back into lakes and oceans.

A flooded street in India makes getting around difficult!

Rain and us

We need rain because we all need water to drink. Farmers need rain for their crops and animals. Some places get more rain than others. Hilly and mountainous areas usually have more rain than low-lying, flat areas. This is because as air rises over mountains, it cools down. The water vapour condenses, falling as rain or snow. Heavy rain can sometimes cause flooding, but if a place has no rainfall for a long time, land and rivers can dry up and cause a **drought.** Deserts can go for months or even years without rain.

A drought has caused a river bed to dry out and the earth to crack.

Seasonal rains

Some parts of the world, including parts of Africa, Asia, Australia, South America and North America, have heavy seasonal or **monsoon** rains that arrive after weeks of hot, dry weather. They arrive when winds that are blowing from the land change direction to carry moist air from the ocean onto the land.

? How do clouds tell us whether it is going to be rainy or fine weather? Turn the page to find out.

Clouds

Clouds can tell us what kind of weather to expect. We can learn to spot rain clouds and tell then apart from fine weather clouds. Small, white and puffy clouds (1) or high wispy clouds (2) mean fine weather. Huge, puffy, white clouds (3) can mean a short period of heavy rain and dark, dense clouds (4) can bring storms. Flat, grey clouds (5) mean drizzle or light rain.

1. Cumulus

2. Cirrus

3. Cumulonimbus

4. Nimbostratus

5. Stratus

The different colored bands in a rainbow over a village in Mexico.

Rainbows

If the Sun shines when it is raining we may see a rainbow. Sunlight looks white but it is actually made up of different colors. As the Sun's rays shine through a raindrop, the different colored light rays bend and separate so we see all the colors that make up sunlight as a rainbow.

TRY THIS

Cut the top section off a clear plastic bottle that has a flat bottom. Draw lines on the bottle, marking 1-inch (2.5 cm) sections, starting at the bottom. Place the bottle outside to catch the rain (you may need to push it into the ground a little so it doesn't fall over). Record the daily amounts on a bar graph. Remember to empty the bottle each day.

QUIZ TIME!

How many colors can you see in a rainbow?

a. 5
b. 7
c. more than 100

Answer on page 32.

Make This

The **Aztec** people thought that using a rainstick could bring on a rainstorm. Your own rainstick will make the sound of falling rain.

1

Draw around the end of a cardboard tube onto a piece of white card stock. Repeat to make a second circle.

2

Cut out the two circles, but cut a half-inch (1 cm) larger than the line you have drawn. Make lots of tabs by snipping from the edge to the line.

3

Tape one of the circles to one end of the tube. Use the tabs to overlap the end of the tube. Make sure it is stuck down tightly.

4

Scrunch some newspaper squares into balls. Add these and a handful of rice into the tube. Tape the other card stock circle tightly to the open end of the tube.

5

Cut a piece of colored paper to fit around your tube. Tape in place and decorate it with paint, string and feathers.

Tip your rainstick onto one end. The rice moving through the tube should sound like rain!

SNOWY WEATHER

Snow and ice can form when the temperature falls below freezing.

When the temperature falls below 32°F (0°C), moisture in clouds can freeze. Sometimes water droplets freeze into sleet as they fall, or become freezing rain, which freezes as it touches the cold ground. If water droplets are carried up by drafts of air inside clouds, when they meet cold air they can turn into hailstones or snowflakes. As more water vapor freezes around them, the frozen droplets become bigger and heavier until they begin to fall as hail or snow.

Polar bears live on the ice in the Arctic. They are adapted to live in cold places.

QUIZ TIME!
What color is a polar bear's fur?

a. blue

b. white

c. It has no color.

Answer on page 32.

Snowy places

Mountains and other high places, and areas that lie within the polar circles get the most snowfall. In the Arctic and Antarctic, there is snow and ice all year round. The animals that live here are adapted to living in the cold. Polar bears (left) live in the Arctic. They have a thick layer of fat under their skin, thick fur, and they even have fur on the bottom of their paws. The **Inuit** people of the Arctic are also used to living with the snow. They use snow sleds, **snowmobiles** and skis to get around.

Snowstorms

Snowstorms can bring heavy snow. If it is also windy the snow can blow into blizzards, making it hard to see. Heavy snow can cause problems for transportation and farmers. But snow can also be fun for people who enjoy winter sports, such as sledding, skiing and snowboarding.

Quick FACTS

• Snow, ice, sleet, hail and frost can all form when the temperature falls below freezing.
• Snow can can be a lot of fun!

? How many sides does a snowflake have? Turn the page to find out.

Inuit hunters sometimes use snowmobiles to pull sleds around on the ice and snow.

SNOWIEST PLACES

The top 5 snowiest places in the world are

1. **Mount Rainier, Washington**
2. **Niseko, Japan**
3. **Mount Fidelity, Glacier National Park, Canada**
4. **Alta ski area, Utah**
5. **Alyeska, Alaska**

Lots of tiny ice crystals make up these beautiful snowflakes.

Frost

Frost forms when the air temperature falls below freezing and water vapor in the air freezes into ice crystals on a cold surface, such as plant leaves or a window. When there is enough moisture in the air, it can cause ice crystals to grow and cluster into a **hoar frost**.

The ice crystals in a hoar frost cover the branches of a tree.

Snowflakes

Snowflakes form when moisture in clouds begins to freeze around tiny bits of pollen or dust in the air to form ice crystals. As they begin to fall, more water vapor freezes around them, forming clusters of ice crystals that make snowflakes. Snowflakes have six sides, but each one is different and can be made from up to 200 ice crystals. They look white because of the way light reflects off the crystals.

TRY THIS Leave a piece of black paper in the freezer and put it outside when it snows. Use a magnifying glass to examine the snowflakes that fall on it.

Make This

There might not be any real snow in a snow globe, but you can have lots of fun making a wintry scene. You could make one to celebrate Christmas!

When you shake the snow globe you become the wind moving the snow. What happens when you shake it gently? What happens if you shake it a bit harder?

1 Press some modeling clay into the bottom of a clean glass jar. Add a plastic figure (or an object such as a tree).

2 Ask an adult to fill the jar with baby oil. Add some glitter. (Make sure you add enough as this will be the "snow.")

3 Put on the lid. The lid must be on tight! Ask an adult to help you seal it with some more modeling clay or a hot glue gun.

4 The glitter will settle at the bottom of the glass jar. Shake it gently to make the snow begin to swirl.

WINDY WEATHER

Wind is moving air. Warm air rises and cool air sinks; this movement creates the wind.

Warm and cool air

When the Sun shines, the air near the ground gets warmer. Warm air rises because it is lighter and less dense than cool air. Cooler air comes in below it to take its place. This movement of the air creates the wind.

A strong wind by the sea has blown these deck chairs inside out.

Windy days

Huge waves, caused by windy weather, crash over a lighthouse.

We can't see the wind, but we can feel it when it blows in our faces or hair. When we are out on a windy day, it can be hard to hold onto hats or umbrellas, and we can even find it difficult to walk against a strong wind. We can also see how windy weather affects things around us. It blows through trees and bushes and makes them lose their leaves and even their branches. It can also make lakes and seas rough or choppy, bringing big waves onto the seashore.

A windsock traps the wind, showing its strength and direction.

Measuring winds

Winds are named after the direction they blow from. So a north wind blows from the north and a south wind from the south. Wind socks are used at airports and other places to show how strong the wind is and which direction it is blowing from. The speed of the wind can be measured using an **anemometer.** When it is placed in the wind, the arms on the anemometer spin, showing the wind speed. Weather forecasters describe wind conditions using the Beaufort wind force scale. It measures wind strength on a scale of 0 to 12.

The cups on the arms of this anemometer catch the wind and make it spin.

BEAUFORT WIND FORCE SCALE

0=calm
1=light air
2=light breeze
3=gentle breeze
4=moderate breeze
5=fresh breeze
6=strong breeze
7=near gale
8=gale
9=strong gale
10=storm
11=violent storm
12=hurricane

QUIZ TIME!

When the weather is very windy we somtimes say it is...

a. blustery
b. breezy
c. gentle

Answer on page 32.

? Which places do you think are the most windy? Turn the page to find out.

Windy places

We feel the wind most in open places, such as fields, hilltops and by the sea, where it can blow without anything blocking its way. Buildings, trees and hedges act as windbreaks, and where there are mountains, wind often blows into the valleys that lie between them.

Kite surfers enjoy windy weather at a beach in Wissant, France.

A dust storm in the Sahara desert.

Winds of the world

There are different types of wind around the world. Monsoon winds change direction, blowing from either the oceans or the land to bring wet and dry seasons. The Sirocco is a hot, dusty wind that blows from the Sahara desert. The Mistral is a cold, dry north wind that blows in southern France in the winter or spring.

The wind and us

Strong winds can sometimes cause problems for transport. High bridges and even roads may have to close when winds are dangerously strong. But the wind can also bring people fun when they enjoy outdoor sports like sailing, windsurfing, hang gliding or kite surfing.

Quick FACTS

• Winds are named after the direction from which they blow.
• They are measured from 0–12 on a wind scale called the Beaufort wind force scale.
• Open spaces are often the windiest places.

Make This

The arrow on a weather vane always points in the direction the wind is blowing from. So if it is pointing to the S then there is a southerly wind.

Take your vane outside. Use a compass to make sure the N on the weather vane is pointing to the north. Watch it move when the wind changes direction.

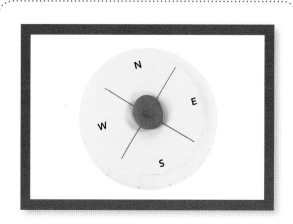

1 Paint the back of a paper plate. When dry, divide it into N, E, S, and W. Place some modeling clay in its center.

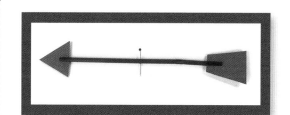

3 Cut a triangle and a tail shape from card stock. (Make the triangle smaller than the tail.) Cut a slot in each end of a straw and push the shapes into the slots.

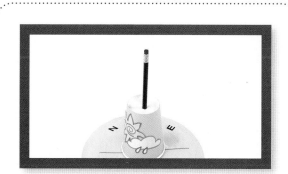

2 Glue a paper cup onto the plate, over the modeling clay. Push a pencil (with an eraser on the end) through the cup and into the modeling clay, as shown.

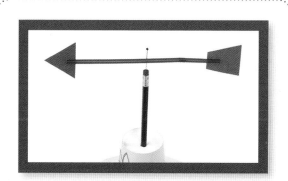

4 Carefully push a pin through the straw and into the eraser. It should be able to swivel around freely on top.

TIP: If your weather vane blows over in the wind, weigh it down with more modeling clay or hold it down with pebbles.

STORMY WEATHER

Stormy weather can bring floods, strong winds, thunder and lightning.

Floods

When heavy rain falls for a long time, rivers may flood. This means they become so full that they overflow their banks. Flooding can also be caused by high tides and strong winds along coastlines, or when so much rain has fallen that the soil cannot soak up any more water and it can't drain away through underground rocks.

TRY THIS
Collect some pinecones and place them outside or on a window sill. Watch what happens to the cones when the weather is dry and when it turns wet or stormy.

A city street is completely flooded after a tropical rainstorm.

Wild winds

Hurricanes and tornadoes are powerful storms with strong, damaging winds. Hurricanes are called typhoons and cyclones in different parts of the world. They form over warm oceans, when strong winds blow together, forcing warm moist air upwards. When they reach land, they bring heavy rain, strong winds and huge waves that can damage buildings, trees and cars.

A hurricane lashes palm trees and a beach in Miami, Florida.

A tornado forms over land when a column of warm moist air rises quickly. As the air rises and mixes with colder air, differences in wind speed and direction can make it rotate or twist. It gets faster and faster as it draws in more warm air. Water droplets in the moist air condense into rain or hail, and the cloud forms a funnel shape. If the funnel cloud touches the ground, it becomes a tornado.

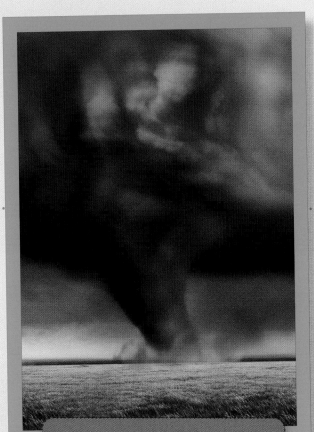

A tornado touching the ground, destroying the crops in a farmer's field.

FACTS

• When warm air rises very quickly over sea or land and meets cooler air, super storms called hurricanes and tornadoes can form.
• Storms can damage things, such as crops, and cause flooding.

? What do you think causes thunder and lightning? Turn the page to find out.

Thunder and lightning

Thunderstorms happen when warm moist air rises suddenly and quickly, forming dark, puffy clouds that carry on growing and rising. As the warm air meets much cooler air, water vapor inside the clouds turns to water droplets, hail and ice crystals. They bump into each other as they are carried up and down by drafts of air. This bumping creates **charges** of electricity in the clouds and on the ground below them. When these charges connect, they form an electric current and release heat and energy that we see as a flash of lightning.

Lightning flows between clouds or from a cloud to the ground. It heats the air violently, making it expand so quickly that as it cools it explodes with a booming sound, which we hear as thunder. We see lightning before we hear thunder because light travels much faster than sound.

QUIZ TIME!
What is a flash of lightning called?

a. a blizzard

b. a blaze

c. a bolt

Answer on page 32.

Make This

You can make a lightning cracker to create your own thunder! It squashes the air to produce a cracking sound when you flick it downwards.

You can decorate your cracker with lightning patterns. Experiment by making crackers using thinner or thicker paper. Which type of paper works best?

1

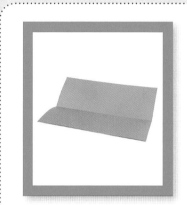

Fold a sheet of paper in half, lengthways. Open it out and lay it flat.

2

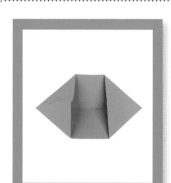

Fold each of the four corners in so the points touch the center line as shown.

3

Fold in half again, along the center fold. The opening should be facing you.

4

Fold in half again so the points meet. Then open it out again.

5

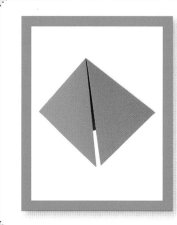

Fold the two top corners down as shown. It should make a diamond shape.

6

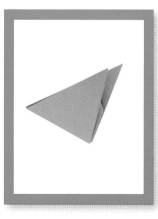

Fold it back on itself so the two points are facing you. Hold the two points and flick the cracker down, hard.

GLOSSARY

anemometer a device for measuring the speed and force of the wind

atmosphere the mixture of gases that surround the Earth

axis an imaginary line through the center of an object

Aztec the native peoples of Mexico from the 13th to 16th centuries CE

charge a buildup of electrical energy

condenses turns from gas to liquid

contracts gets smaller

deciduous a type of tree or plant that loses its leaves each year

dense heavy and thick

desert a place with very little or no rainfall and few plants

drought a long period with little or no rain

equator the area around the center of the Earth where it is warm all year

evergreen a type of tree or plant that keeps its leaves all year

evaporate turn from liquid into gas

expands gets bigger

forecasters in this instance, a person who predicts the weather

fronts the edge of a moving mass of warm or cold air

hemisphere half of the Earth, either north or south of the equator

hoar frost large clusters of ice crystals that form on plants and other surfaces

Inuit the native peoples

of northern Canada, Greenland and Alaska

migrate to change habitat, moving from one region to another

monsoon seasonal winds that change direction, to bring wet or dry seasons

orbit to travel around something

polar circles the Arctic and Antarctic areas, around the north and south poles

pollinate to carry pollen to a plant to fertilize it

snowmobile a small motor vehicle with skis for traveling over snow

symbols objects or pictures that represent something else

temperate belonging to the temperate zones, between the tropics and the polar circles

thermometer instrument that measures temperature

tropical belonging to the tropics, the areas above and below the equator, between the Tropics of Cancer and Capricorn

water vapor moisture in the air

BOOKS

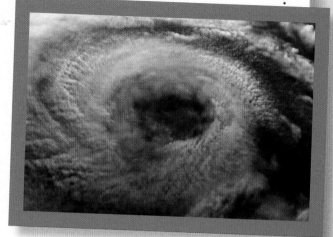

Air and Weather
by Barbara Davis (Gareth Stevens
Publishing , 2007)

All About the Weather
by Edward Close (PowerKids Press, 2014)

The Changing Seasons **(series)**
by Paul Humphrey (Franklin Watts , 2012)

Earth Cycles: Seasons by Sally Morgan
(Franklin Watts, 2012)

Project Geography: Weather
by Sally Hewitt (Franklin Watts, 2013)

Popcorn: Science Corner: Weather and Seasons
by Alice Harman (Wayland, 2013)

WEBSITES

Due to the changing nature of Internet links, PowerKids Press has developed
an online list of websites related to the subject of this book. This site is
updated regularly. Please use this link to access the list:
www.powerkidslinks.com/mal/was/

INDEX

QUIZ ANSWERS

Page 7. b – counterclockwise

Page 8. b – pigments

Page 16. c – over 100. There are seven main colors in a rainbow (red, orange, yellow, green, blue, indigo and violet), but the human eye can actually see over 100 shades of these colors!

Page 18. c – it has no color. (Polar bears look white because their fur reflects the color of the snow.)

Page 24. a – blustery

Page 28. c – a bolt